Presented to:

_____

Presented by:

_____

Date:

_____

the HIGHEST CALL

RESOLVE *in the* MIDST *of* SACRIFICE

ELM HILL BOOKS

The Highest Call: Resolve in the Midst of Sacrifice
©2003 ELM HILL BOOKS, an imprint of J. Countryman®,
a division of Thomas Nelson, Inc., Nashville TN 37214
ISBN: 1-4041-8463-5

Manuscript written and compiled by Jan White and Beth Ryan
Manuscript edited by Rebecca Currington
in conjunction with Snapdragon Editorial Group, Inc.

The quoted ideas expressed in this book (but not Scripture verses) are not, in all cases, exact quotations, as some have been edited for clarity and brevity. In all cases, the author has attempted to maintain the speaker's original intent. In some cases, quoted material for this book was obtained from secondary sources, primarily print media. While every effort was made to ensure the accuracy of these sources, the accuracy cannot be guaranteed. For additions, deletions, corrections, or clarifications in future editions of this text, please write ELM HILL BOOKS.

Scripture quotations marked NCV are taken from the *International Children's Bible®, New Century Version®*. Copyright © 1986, 1988, 1999 by Tommy Nelson®, a division of Thomas Nelson, Inc., Nashville, Tennessee 37214. Used by permission.

Scripture quotations marked NKJV are taken from *The Holy Bible, New King James Version*. Copyright © 1982 by Thomas Nelson, Inc. Used by permission.

Scripture quotations marked NRSV are taken from *The New Revised Standard Version Bible*. Copyright © 1989 by the Division of Christian Education of the Churches of Christ in the United States of America and are used by permission.

Scripture quotations marked NIV are taken from the *Holy Bible, New International Version*, (North American Edition)®. Copyright 1973, 1978, 1984 by International Bible Society. Used by permission of Zondervan Publishing House. All rights reserved.

Scripture quotations marked GNT are taken from *The Good News Bible, Second Edition, Today's English Version*. Copyright © 1992 by American Bible Society. Used by permission. All rights reserved.

Scripture quotations marked KJV are taken from the *King James Version* of the Bible.

INTRODUCTION

Jesus said, "Greater love has
no one than this, than to lay down
one's life for his friends."

JOHN 15:13 NKJV

More than twenty-five million American veterans are living today. Many of these courageous men and women, like those who went before them, have faced death and suffered unimaginable hardships while fighting to protect our freedoms and safeguard our inalienable rights of "life, liberty, and the pursuit of happiness."

From the shores of Omaha Beach and the jungles of Vietnam, to the sands of the Persian Gulf, the mountains of Afghanistan and Iraq, and many other harsh battlefields around the world, these American heroes have protected our homeland and liberated millions in foreign lands.

America's greatness is endowed by our Creator and preserved because of the heroes who serve every day, whether in the military or in public service. They all answer the highest call by regularly placing their own lives at risk for others.

We, the American people, owe a deep debt of gratitude to all those who've accepted the highest call. To those of you who bear scars, seen and unseen, to your families who equally sacrificed, and to the fallen who gave the "greatest love," we salute you and dedicate this book to you!

TABLE OF CONTENTS

My deep desire and hope is that I shall never fail in my duty, but that at all times, and especially right now, I shall be full of courage, so that with my whole being I shall bring honor to Christ, whether I live or die.

PHILIPPIANS 1:20 GNT

HONOR DUE

We don't have to turn to our history books for heroes. They are all around us.

PRESIDENT RONALD REAGAN
STATE OF THE UNION ADDRESS
JANUARY 26, 1982

Whether you're retired from the military, presently serving in one of the branches of the armed forces, or living each day protecting and serving in the local communities of the United States of America, you are to be honored for your brave sacrifice.

Your unwavering fortitude and resolve to protect the freedoms that are held dear by every American will forever impact our nation. Your individual name may not be written on the pages of American history books, but your spirit, sacrifice, and determination have written history and preserved *freedom!*

Perhaps President George W. Bush said it best:

Your courage, your willingness to face danger for your country and for each other made this day possible. Because of you, our nation is more secure. Our commitment to liberty is America's tradition—declared at our founding, affirmed in Franklin Roosevelt's Four Freedoms, asserted in the Truman Doctrine and in Ronald Reagan's challenge to an evil empire. In the words of the prophet Isaiah: "To the captives, 'Come out,' and to those in darkness, 'Be free.'"

Thank you for serving our country and our cause.

HONORING OUR VETERANS

Webster defines *veteran* as a former member of the armed forces. But a more deserving definition might read: "A person who has laid aside personal freedoms and served in the armed forces in order to ensure the liberty and inalienable rights that all Americans enjoy."

This is the amazing story of one such *veteran*:

On February 12, 1973, Americans watched and waited as news coverage told of the first plane landing at Clark Air Force Base in the Philippines, bringing our POWs home from North Vietnam. Captain Jeremiah Denton, the highest ranking soldier on that first flight from captivity, was informed that he might be expected to speak for the POWs with him.

When he stepped off the plane, Denton walked slowly down the ramp. Seeing the American flag, he saluted and said these memorable words: "We are honored to have had the opportunity to serve our country under difficult circumstances. We are profoundly grateful to our commander in chief and to our nation for this day. God bless America."

Jeremiah Denton spoke on behalf of his fellow POWs not only that day, but also during his imprisonment. During a televised interview on May 17, 1966, he repeatedly blinked his eyes as though the lights for the cameras were too bright for him. But it was discovered that Jeremiah Denton had actually been blinking the message, T-O-R-T-U-R-E in Morse code.

For seven years and seven months, Denton suffered severe mistreatment as a prisoner of war. Four years of his captivity were spent in solitary confinement.

At the time he was shot down in 1965, Jeremiah Denton was a commander. While a prisoner of war he was promoted to the rank of captain. In April 1974, shortly after his release, he was promoted to rear admiral, and then in 1980 he was elected to the U.S. Senate.

*Weeping may endure
for a night, but joy comes
in the morning.*

PSALM 30:5 NKJV

STOLEN HONOR

Many veterans who fought courageously in the Vietnam War came home to angry protestors who spat, cursed, and expressed disdain. The honor and respect they so richly deserved was denied them by the politics of an unpopular war and those who had no appreciation for the sacrifice that had been made on their behalf.

With time, even the Americans who passionately objected to the war recognized the wrong done to these gallant men and women. More than 240 Medals of Honor, America's highest reward for military valor, were presented to those who served in Vietnam. More than half were awarded posthumously.

Many of those to whom the medals were awarded gave their lives in a specific act of selfless heroism—they threw their bodies over live grenades to save the lives of their fellow soldiers. As the award specifies, these brave men and women performed acts of such conspicuous gallantry as to rise "above the call of duty."

TRIBUTE TO THE VIETNAM VETERAN

Over 2.6 million served
Over 58,000 gave their lives
They fought for their country
They fought for freedom
They fought with honor
In the end they fought for each other
Harsh words from home
and difficult memories have faded
But their legacy has not
WE WILL REMEMBER!

CHILDREN OF VIETNAM VETERANS

WRITTEN BY TODD CLEGG

OUR FALLEN HEROES

1st Lt. John F. Cochrane articulated the feelings of many in this letter to his parents while serving in Vietnam:

Dear Folks,

We have our troubles in America, but what little of the world I have seen doesn't hold a candle to what our country is. Now you may think this is all written in a highly emotional state, and if fear is considered a highly emotional state, and it is, then you are right. But I have sat here this night and looked into the faces of eighteen young men—the oldest is twenty-eight—and I have talked to them about their homes and families and wives and sweethearts.

Every one of these kids knows what he wants. There is not a "hero" in the group over here looking for glory or medals or any of that other garbage— they are here because they felt they were needed, that's all! ... I could feel the tension they were feeling as they asked me what they should do—or where the machine guns should be employed. I was scared—not because of death, because I have accepted the Lord and I know where I will spend eternity—but because I also had to assume the responsibility for eighteen other lives—and that takes guts—lots of them.

It is morning, a Sunday morning, the troops are going around with a silly grin on their faces, mocking the fear that gripped them so hard last night. It's over now, and they know it. The front that each of us puts up to hide our inner feelings is once again in place.

I have put the word out that reinforcements are on the way, and we will be able to move back to camp when they arrive. Laughter, the thing that was so plainly missing last night, is heard now. Man is now back in his element. He can see what is going on around him. He would go into battle during daylight much the same as he would do any other job. But at night, like last night, even if there are a hundred of you, you are alone—just the soldier and the dark and the unknown enemy.

On October 24, 1966, nine days after this letter was written, 1st Lt. John F. Cochrane died in combat. His letter has been most precious to his family. And it should be precious to all of us, because it informs us of the unique terrors and remarkable courage shown by those who served in a war that literally changed the rules of engagement. They served and sacrificed for all Americans. They courageously did their duty, answering the *highest call*.

Though we may not be able to see His purpose or His plan, the Lord of heaven is on His throne and in firm control of the universe and our lives. So we entrust Him with our future. We entrust Him with our very lives.

MAX LUCADO

AMERICA LOOKS UP

I am persuaded that neither death nor life, nor angels nor principalities nor powers, nor things present nor things to come, nor height nor depth, nor any other created thing, shall be able to separate us from the love of God which is in Christ Jesus our Lord.

ROMANS 8:38–39 NKJV

BEYOND THE CALL OF DUTY

*Duty is the sublimest
word in our language.
Do your duty in all things.
You cannot do more,
you should never do less.*

ROBERT E. LEE

MAY THE GLORY FOREVER RING

You may be a veteran of WWI or WWII. Or you may have served in Korea, Vietnam, or the Persian Gulf. You may have been called upon to fight the battle for freedom against terrorism and tyranny on soil far from home. You may even have served your country during peacetime, adding might to the words of our diplomats and a united front to those who would wish to do us harm. Whenever and wherever you served, you almost certainly left your family, friends, job—your life—behind to do your duty. You are a HERO!

We remember these who served freedom's cause:

WW1—4,734,991 served and 116,516 died

WWII—16,112,566 served and 405,399 died

Korean War—5,720,000 served and 36,568 died

Vietnam War—8,744,000 served and 58,203 died

Persian Gulf War—235 total deaths as of March 15, 2003

War on Terrorism—64 total deaths as of March 15, 2003

Operation Iraqi Freedom—139 total deaths as of May 1, 2003

They heard our country's call. They went forth and counted not their own lives dear, but offered them gladly in humanity's name—for God and for right. It is our duty to be proud of them. The greatest war in the history of the world closed August 14, 1945, when the warring nations laid down their arms. The Germans, Japanese, and all their allies lay prostrate, defeated—they who knew no mercy and had violated every law of humanity and civilization. They begged for mercy, but the *victory was ours!* While history may overlook many of the brave deeds of our gallant men and women, their memory will ever live in the hearts and minds of freedom-loving people of this great nation. The heart of every true American, must needs throb with wondrous pride as they honor the immortal American heroes who have fought for freedom's cause. For those who died in the service and others who are now gone, the honor and glory is theirs. For those who offered all and still live, *may the glory forever ring.*

MAJOR BOYD FALLWELL
CHAPLAIN U.S. ARMY,
VOLUNTEER RESERVE

WHY, GOD?

Why, O LORD, do you
stand far off? Why do you hide
yourself in times of trouble?

PSALM 10:1 NIV

In his book, *Why God?* Charles Swindoll
offered the following words:

The date, September 11, 2001, is forever etched
in our national memory. That morning stands as the
never-to-be-forgotten hour when time stood still as
we stared in horror and disbelief. With calculated
and unconscionable malice, beastly terrorists
stabbed our nation repeatedly in the heart—the
World Trade Center in New York, at the Pentagon in
Washington, and along a quiet countryside in south-
west Pennsylvania. Thousands of unsuspecting civil-

ians were brutally murdered. Our fellow Americans bled and died. Now we are, once again, at war as a nation. Our enemy is demonic and deceitful. Though identified by the frightening sounding name "terrorism," he is a coward to the core.

We witnessed on September 11 the limitless depths to which he will go to bring us down. But America will neither fear nor fail. We will not consider any sacrifice too great or any cost too high. Because we know that in the end God always wins, we know we will win. Let us walk directly into the sneer of the enemy with relentless resolve. Let us kneel before the Lord our Sovereign God with fresh faith. Let us trust Him through Jesus Christ our Savior with repentant hearts, quiet confidence, and absolute dependence. By doing these things, we can be certain of the final outcome, as the Psalmist once declared: "Through God we shall do valiantly" (Psalm 60:12 KJV). Still, in our heart of hearts we whisper, "Why, God?"

WHAT IS A HERO?

On September 11, 2001, Americans watched in horror as two jetliners flew into the Twin Towers of New York's World Trade Center and another crashed into the Pentagon in Washington, D.C. In the minutes and hours that followed, brave souls united in their resolve to protect and rescue. From the *first responders* to the regular citizens to the military personnel who stood guard over our skies and borders, many went above the call of duty and answered the *highest call*.

These were not the superheroes of fantasy and fiction. They were ordinary people—husbands and wives, fathers and mothers, sons and daughters, friends and colleagues. Quietly, courageously, they called upon God for help and rose to the occasion, many risking death to help others from the rubble.

They are the brave, the valiant, the *heroes*.

FIRST RESPONDERS

Long before the Twin Towers collapsed and the Pentagon suffered a grievous wound, true heroes have been hard at work across the country, in small towns and large cities, day in and day out, defending and protecting America's citizens. They are America's firefighters, police officers, and emergency medical personnel. They are known as *first responders*. Like our military, they are willing to risk their lives to serve others.

★

Within a single hour, more than three hundred firefighters were lost. And our nation still mourns. They did not live to know who had caused the destruction or why. They only knew their duty. And that was to go in, to follow the faintest cry, to search for the trapped and hopeless, and to save those who could be saved.

PRESIDENT GEORGE W. BUSH

Firefighters and paramedics were among the first to answer the call of duty in New York City on September 11, 2001. Some 343 of those who came to save lives lost their own when the towers collapsed. Later, it was determined that 60 of those fallen firefighters had been off duty that day.

Some were at home resting after long shifts, while others were reporting to second jobs, needed to supplement their income. But, regardless of where they were when the alarms were sounded, those sixty fearless men and women responded without hesitation.

Those fearless *first responders* who came to the aid of New York's citizens on September 11 and those who responded on an infamous April morning in Oklahoma City—in fact, all those who respond to crises of lesser magnitude on a daily basis have all courageously walked out the tenets of the Firefighters Pledge:

> I promise concern for others—a willingness to help all those in need.
> I promise courage—courage to face and conquer my fears. Courage to share and endure the ordeal of those who need me.
> I promise strength—strength of heart to bear whatever burdens might be placed upon me. Strength of body to deliver to safety all those placed within my care.
> I promise the wisdom to lead, the compassion to comfort, and the love to serve unselfishly whenever I am called.

AUTHOR UNKNOWN

What more excellent way to pay tribute than with these words orchestrated by the son of a fireman:

My dad's a fireman and proud am I indeed,
for he is someone special, whose wisdom I still need.
Dad and I are buddies, and to me that means a lot,
a bond to last forever, with love that's from the heart.
He took me to parades when other kids stayed home,
and he taught me to play baseball on a field without a dome.
He taught me how to fix things, even let me use his tools.
What I learned from my dad can't be learned in school.
The example that he set, I follow every day,
placing God and country first, in showing me the way.
Precious are those years, now tucked away with time,
tenderly remembered; I am the leaf, he is the vine.
Dad, hear me as I say, I love you man-to-man
and I am proud to tell the world,
my dad is a fireman.

In a speech honoring fallen *police officers*, President Bush told about fallen officer, John Perry, who went beyond the call of duty and gave all on September 11, 2001.

Perry retired on that fateful fall morning and turned in his badge at the 40th Precinct. "A moment later, he heard the sound of the first attack and the radio traffic that followed. He put his badge back on and was last seen directing people to safety at the bottom of the tower."

Bush concluded, "No one goes into police work for the money, nor does anybody put on the uniform expecting a life of ease. You take the job because you respect the law and you know that someone has to do the challenging work of enforcing it. Fortunately, this great country—America—has never been short of such men and women and your devoted service, and we are very grateful."

Those who have pledged to enforce the laws of our land, thus ensuring domestic tranquility for our citizens, place themselves in harm's way on a daily basis. They, too, suffered great losses on September 11, 2001. Thirty-seven police officers lost their lives. All those who gave so much on that day—both those who lived and those who died—were honoring the following oath:

The Law Enforcement Oath of Honor

On my honor, I will never betray my badge, my integrity, my character, or the public trust.
I will always have the courage to hold myself and others accountable for our actions.
I will always uphold the constitution, my community, and the agency I serve.

INTERNATIONAL ASSOCIATION
OF CHIEFS OF POLICE

★

I will carry this: It is the police shield of a man named George Howard, who died at the World Trade Center trying to save others. It was given to me by his mom, Arlene, as a proud memorial to her son.

PRESIDENT GEORGE W. BUSH

Let every soul be subject
to the governing authorities.
For there is no authority except
from God, and the authorities
that exist are appointed by God.
For he is God's minister to you
for good. But if you do evil, be
afraid; for he does not bear the
sword in vain; for he is God's
minister, an avenger to execute
wrath on him who practices evil.

ROMANS 13:1,4 NKJV

NO GREATER LOVE

*Jesus said, "A new commandment
I give to you, that you love one
another; as I have loved you, that
you also love one another. By this all
will know that you are My disciples,
if you have love for one another."*

JOHN 13:34-35 NKJV

Consider the love shown by these courageous men who met on the *USS Dorchester* during WWII:

You may not have heard their names—George L. Fox, Alexander D. Goode, John P. Washington, and Clark V. Polling. They were chaplains—one Protestant, one Jewish, and two Catholic. On the surface these men could not have been more different. There was the country boy from Vermont, the city boy from Washington, the slum kid from Newark, and the minister's son from New York City. But underneath, they shared the same heart of love for God and their fellowman.

George Fox had served as a medical corps assistant in World War I. He received a Silver Star for bravery for rescuing a wounded soldier on a battlefield filled with poison gas. He had no gas mask. Fox came home to Vermont and became a public accountant. Later, he felt led to study for the ministry. When world war came again, he told his wife and two children, "I've got to go. I know what our boys are about to face."

Alexander Goode had planned to follow in his father's footsteps and become a rabbi. Growing up in the Washington, D.C. area, he walked fifteen miles to Arlington Cemetery out of respect to see the interment of the Unknown Soldier. He did become a rabbi, but felt unworthy. Goode thought he could help heal men's souls if he knew how to heal their bodies, so he got a medical degree. He left his wife and four children to serve his country in World War II.

Clark V. Polling, the youngest chaplain, was the seventh generation in an unbroken line of ministers. A Presbyterian pastor in Schenectady, New York, when war came along, he didn't want to serve as a chaplain, believing he should defend his country with arms. But after a conversation with his father, Polling became a chaplain, leaving his wife and little girl to sail on the Dorchester. He told his father, "Dad, don't pray for my safe return. Just pray that I shall do my duty."

John P. Washington, the son of Irish immigrants from Newark, New Jersey, grew up in a poor family with nine mouths to feed. He sold newspapers to help his family's income. Johnny, as he was known, sang in his church choir and was the leader of the South Twelfth Street Boys in Newark. Washington chose the priesthood and later organized baseball teams for boys in his parish. When war came and some of his boys went into the army, Father Johnny went along with them.

On that fateful day, February 2, 1943, at 12:55 A.M. about 150 miles from Greenland, a torpedo from a U-223 ripped into the Dorchester's right side. An old ship brought out of mothballs for the war, the Dorchester immediately began to sink. The four chaplains took charge of handing out life vests and let others board the lifeboats. Survivors recall seeing the four standing on the deck, their arms linked, praying for the safety of the men escaping the ship into icy waters.

In his book, *Why God?* Charles Swindoll quoted these words about the kind of love referred to in John 15:13 KJV: *Greater love hath no man than this, that a man lay down his life for his friends.*

It's the kind of love that lets a man put his two-month-old child into someone else's arms, so he can try to help make sure that the doomed aircraft he is riding on is not used as a flying bomb. The kind of love that makes a firefighter run into a teetering skyscraper in the hope that he can rescue the people trapped inside, only to have that building collapse on him and more than a hundred of his brother firefighters.

This country, and the free world beside us, stood shocked and dismayed. We are angry, and justifiably so. We have been attacked by people with no desire but to make us afraid, to make us hurt, perhaps even to make us hate the way they do. I know that whatever their ultimate goals, they have failed already. They attempted to sow fear, and instead reaped heroism.

In his book, *When Tragedy Strikes*, Charles Stanley wrote these words.

When I was about nine years of age, Pearl Harbor was attacked. The American response was unforgettable. Young men, barely sixteen or seventeen years old, lined up to enlist and to serve. They did not care which branch of service would take them; they only wanted to defend their nation. When united, this country trembles before no other power. We have a national sense of courage and bravery.

When we, as individuals or as a nation, stand sovereign under the protection of God, then we can be assured that He will not fail us. No matter neither the disaster that we face nor the enemy at our gate, with our God we will be triumphant. Only in eternity will we understand some of the mysterious ways of almighty God. Only then will we grasp the significance of His eternal plan that encompasses all of us.

DEATH—THE VANQUISHED FOE

While we cannot guarantee the safety of our children, or ourselves, or anyone else in this life, Jesus Christ does guarantee our safety in eternity. When you and I place our faith in Him as our Savior and yield our lives to Him as Lord, God promises that we "shall not perish but have eternal life" (John 3:16 NIV).

ANNE GRAHAM LOTZ

HEAVEN: MY FATHER'S HOUSE

Death is the one human experience that shows no partiality. In the recent war with Iraq, media reports continually flowed showing soldiers who were standing in line waiting to be baptized because they recognized that death must come to everyone and for them it might be sooner rather than later. The truth is, they wanted to be sure just where their life after death would be and they found that comfort from the promise Christ gave in His Word.

Jesus said, "Let not your heart be troubled; you believe in God, believe also in Me. In My Father's house are many mansions; if it were not so, I would have told you. I go to prepare a place for you."

JOHN 14:1-2 NKJV

MILITARY HONOR BURIAL CEREMONY

Major Boyd Fallwell, Chaplain for the U.S. Army, Volunteer Reserve, uses this moving ceremony for military honor burials:

We are assembled here to give a last tribute of respect and affection to a departed comrade. The years toll by as the ranks of our veterans diminish. One by one our comrades leave us, one by one they join that company of heroic men and women who have defended our country under arms. With the help of God they have kept America free, for you and for me, so that we truly can be "one nation under God."

Departed comrade, veteran of war, well done. The warfare is past, the battle is fought, the battle is won, thou are crowned at last.

This flag we call Old Glory always shines brightly, because it acquires its brilliance from the American veterans who have fought and died to preserve it. It seems to me that our flag shines even brighter today as we honor an American veteran. The love and devotion he/she gave to our beloved country is the reason we are giving military honors.

Day is done, gone the sun,
From the hills, from the lake,
From the sky.
All is well, safely rest,
God is nigh.

Thanks and praise, for our days,
'Neath the sun, 'neath the stars,
'Neath the sky,
As we go, this we know,
God is nigh.

The flag spread on top of the coffin is then folded carefully with white–gloved, calculated hand movements and presented to the veteran's loved one with these words:

This flag was folded very carefully as it is precious to the America people. Since the Revolutionary War forty-eight million Americans have served under this flag and over one million of those have died on the battlefields or were lost at sea. They were defending the freedom that this flag represents. This flag is our nation's very highest honor—there is none higher. It is presented to you on behalf of a grateful nation and the American veterans who have fought and died to preserve it. It is given in memory of your loved one by the United States of America. It is in acknowledgement of his/her honorable and faithful service to our beloved country.

On behalf of the president of the United States of America, I present you with your loved one's flag.

The LORD is my shepherd; I shall not want. He makes me to lie down in green pastures; He leads me beside the still waters. He restores my soul; He leads me in the paths of righteousness for His name's sake.

Yea, though I walk through the valley of the shadow of death, I will fear no evil; for You are with me; Your rod and Your staff, they comfort me.

You prepare a table before me in the presence of my enemies; You anoint my head with oil; My cup runs over. Surely goodness and mercy shall follow me all the days of my life; and I will dwell in the house of the LORD forever.

PSALM 23 NKJV

THE HIGHEST CALL

Let this mind be in you which was also in Christ Jesus, who, being in the form of God, did not consider it robbery to be equal with God, but made Himself of no reputation, taking the form of a bondservant, and coming in the likeness of men. And being found in appearance as a man, He humbled Himself and became obedient to the point of death, even the death of the cross.

PHILIPPIANS 2:5-8 NKJV

THE CROSS AT GROUND ZERO

Amidst the death and destruction at Ground Zero, a construction worker found a remarkable twenty-foot cross. It was made of steel beams and laying in the smoke and rubble. Somehow when the Twin Towers of the World Trade Center collapsed, these beams remained intact, despite intense heat from the jet-fuel inferno.

Frank Silecchia, the former navy man who first saw the cross, told interviewers that the cross symbolized hope and faith, adding that God had not deserted us in this terrible time. Firefighters and police officers engraved the names of their fallen co-workers on the cross, calling it "a way of healing."

★

In the two hundred-plus years since America organized its first fighting units, millions have answered the *highest call*, spilling their blood to protect and defend Americans at home and abroad. But there was only One whose death can pay the price for freedom both now and for eternity. That is Jesus Christ—God's Son. His blood was shed on another cross—the cross of Calvary—for you!

When He answered the *Highest Call*, Jesus Christ reached out His hand to rescue you from death's devastation, to free you from the bondage of sin, to destroy the power of Satan—the enemy of your soul. He gave His all to save you and give you life, liberty, and the hope of happiness. Are you in need of a Savior? Trust Him right now. Feel His loving arms lift you up, and let Him touch and heal your embattled heart. He is standing by, ever waiting to answer your call.

I heard a loud voice from heaven,
saying, "… God will wipe away
every tear from their eyes; there shall
be no more death, nor sorrow, nor
crying. There shall be no more pain,
for the former things have passed
away." Then He who sat on the
throne said, " … It is done! I am the
Alpha and the Omega, the Beginning
and the End. I will give of the
fountain of the water of life freely
to him who thirsts."

REVELATION 21:3-6 NKJV

OUR BLESSED
HERITAGE

America seeks no earthly empire built on blood and force. No ambition, no temptation lures her to thought of foreign dominions. The legions she sends forth are armed, not with the sword, but with the cross. The higher state to which she seeks the allegiance of all mankind is not of human, but of divine origin. She cherishes no other purpose save to merit the favor of Almighty God.

PRESIDENT CALVIN COOLIDGE

There is one word that describes our American flag, and that word is freedom. We do not live under that Nazi Swastika, the flag of the Rising Sun, nor that hammer and sickle, no way. Because of the American veterans, we do live in this free country and we live under this flag. Thank God, this is our red, white, and blue; this is the stars and stripes we teach our young people to honor and respect.

MAJOR BOYD FALLWELL
CHAPLAIN U.S. ARMY,
VOLUNTEER RESERVE

THE STAR SPANGLED BANNER

On Memorial Day weekend at Arlington National Cemetery, small American flags are placed in front of every headstone, as though they were waving a red, white, and blue salute to each individual laid to rest there. These men and women fought and died for the cause of freedom that our flag represents.

Traditionally, the casket of a veteran will be draped with a flag during the funeral. And then, at their gravesite, the military honor guard will precisely fold the flag and present it to his or her grieving survivors.

The Second Continental Congress adopted the Stars and Stripes as the official flag of the United States on June 14, 1777. They wanted a new flag to symbolize a new nation.

George Washington said of the flag, "We take the stars and blue union from heaven, the red from our mother country, separating it by white stripes, thus showing we have separated from her, and the white stripes shall go down to posterity representing liberty."

Francis Scott Key called our flag the "Star-Spangled Banner" when he penned the now famous words of our national anthem in 1814. And we honor our flag in the body of our national pledge:

I pledge allegiance to the flag
of the United States
of America and to the republic
for which it stands,
one nation, under God,
indivisible, with liberty
and justice for all.

The stars upon it were like the bright morning stars of God, and the stripes upon it were beams of morning light. As at early dawn stars shine forth even while it grows light, and then as the sun advances that light breaks into banks and streaming lines of color, the glowing red and intense white striving together, and ribbing the horizon with bars effulgent, so, on the American flag, stars and beams of many-colored light shine out together.

HENRY WARD BEECHER

This flag, which we honor and under which we serve, is the emblem of our unity, our power, our thought and purpose as a nation. It has no other character than which we give it from generation to generation. The choices are ours. It floats in majestic silence about the hosts that execute those choices, whether in peace or in war. And yet, though silent, it speaks to us—speaks to us of our past, of the men and women who went before us, and of the records they wrote upon it.

PRESIDENT WOODROW WILSON

FLAG DAY 1917

ARLINGTON NATIONAL CEMETERY

As far as the eye can see, rows and rows of small white headstones stand, as if at attention, across the landscape of Arlington National Cemetery. One feels the somberness of these hallowed grounds, walking through the gates and along the sidewalks and lanes of its rolling hills.

Every American should have the opportunity to see this eleven-thousand-acre national shrine to those who served and died for the cause of freedom. It's appropriately located in Virginia across the Potomac River from Washington, D.C., where our elected leaders govern this great nation.

More than 260,000 men and women are buried at Arlington National Cemetery—including presidents like John F. Kennedy and William Howard Taft, five-star generals such as Omar Bradley, and countless other soldiers, thousands of them anonymous.

We cannot dedicate, we cannot consecrate, we cannot hallow this ground. The brave men, living and dead, who struggled here, have consecrated it, far above our poor power to add or detract. The world will little note nor long remember what we say here, but it can never forget what they did here. They gave the last full measure of devotion ... that we here highly resolve that these dead shall not have died in vain ... that this nation, under God, shall have a new birth of freedom ... and that government of the people ... by the people ... for the people ... shall not perish from the earth.

PRESIDENT ABRAHAM LINCOLN

GETTYSBURG ADDRESS,

NOVEMBER 19, 1863

TOMB OF THE UNKNOWN SOLDIER

A marble monument sits on a hill in Arlington National Cemetery. The Tomb of the Unknown Soldier was dedicated on Armistice Day, November 11, 1921, when the first unknown soldier of World War I was interred during a solemn ceremony.

Later, in 1931, a fifty-ton piece of Colorado marble was sculpted into the capstone we see today. On the front that faces Washington, D.C., three figures commemorate the spirit of the Allies in World War I. In the center, a female figure stands for "Victory." On the right, a male figure symbolizes "Valor." On the left, "Peace" stands with her palm branch as a reward for the courageous devotion and sacrifice that made the cause of righteousness triumphant.

Carved on the rear panel facing the amphitheater, we read the timeless phrase, "Here Rests in Honored Glory an American Soldier Known but to God."

In a eulogy, President Ronald Reagan spoke for the nation, "The Unknown Soldier who has returned to us today and whom we lay to rest is symbolic of all our missing sons. .... About him, we may well wonder as others have: As a child, did he play in the street in a great American city? Did he work beside his father on a farm in America's heartland? Did he marry? Did he have children? Did he look expectantly to return to a bride?

"Today, we pause to embrace him and all who served us so well. A grateful nation opens her heart today in gratitude for their sacrifice, for their courage, and their noble service. Today we simply say with pride, 'Thank you, dear son, and may God cradle you in His loving arms.'"

UNITED STATES ARMED FORCES OATH OF ENLISTMENT

Every person who enlists in the United States armed forces takes the Oath of Enlistment. Military personnel are responsible for keeping this oath and can be punished should they break it. It reads:

I do solemnly swear (or affirm) that I will support and defend the Constitution of the United States against all enemies, foreign and domestic; that I will bear true faith and allegiance to the same; and that I will obey the orders of the president of the United States and the orders of the officers appointed over me, according to regulations and the Uniform Code of Military Justice. So help me God.

I, the LORD your God, will hold your right hand, saying to you, "Fear not, I will help you."

ISAIAH 41:13 NKJV

THE PURPLE HEART

The Purple Heart is America's oldest military decoration, but one most people would hope and pray they won't receive. It is awarded in the name of the president of the United States to any member of the armed forces, or U.S. civilian, who, while serving in the U.S. Armed Services after April 5, 1917, has been wounded or killed in any action against an enemy of the U.S.

The medal bears the likeness of our founding father, George Washington, upon whose orders it was established originally as a badge of military merit on August 7, 1782. It is to be worn over the left breast.

The Lord is my light and my salvation; whom shall I fear? Though an army may encamp against me, my heart shall not fear; though war may rise against me, in this I will be confident.

PSALM 27:3 NKJV

Only a virtuous people are capable of freedom. As nations become corrupt and vicious, they have more need of masters.

In the beginning of the Contest with Great Britain when we were sensible of danger we had daily prayer in this room for the divine protection. Our prayers, Sir, were heard, and they were graciously answered... And have we now forgotten that powerful friend? Or do we imagine that we no longer need His assistance? I have lived, Sir, a long time, and the longer I live, the more convincing proofs I see of this truth — that God governs the affairs of men. And if a sparrow cannot fall to the ground without His notice, is it probable that an empire can rise without His aid? We have been assured, Sir, in the sacred writings, that "except the Lord build the House they labour in vain that build it."[Psalm 127:1] I firmly believe this; and I also believe that without His concurring aid, we shall succeed in this political building no better than the builders of Babel.

BENJAMIN FRANKLIN — SPEECH AT
THE CONSTITUTIONAL CONVENTION,
JUNE 28, 1787

MY COUNTRY 'TIS OF THEE

My county 'tis of thee,
Sweet land of liberty,
Of thee I sing
Land where my fathers died!
Land of the pilgrim's pride
From every mountain side
Let freedom ring!

Our fathers' God, to Thee,
Author of liberty,
To Thee we sing
Long may our land be bright
With freedom's holy light,
Protect us by Thy might,
Great God, our King